Fishing Success
with
Liquid Crystal
Depthfinders

Fishing Success
with
Liquid Crystal
Depthfinders

by Buck Taylor

Outdoor Skills Bookshelf
Louisville, Alabama

This book is dedicated to my many good friends, and
especially to those who stood by me
in times of trouble.

Contents

Preface

The early African sun licked across the threshold of our small mud hut and flickered through the six-inch window opening near the grass roof. Daylight came almost immediately in the cloudless sky, and I was rather happy to see it. One week before our arrival at the campground, a large male lion had used darkness to march into the cluster of dull, reddish-brown huts, select one in particular and smash the bamboo door into toothpicks with a single blow from his steel-muscled paw.

Grabbing a wild-eyed and startled tourist by the foot, the lion dragged him from his bed and to his death amid cries and pointless pleas for help. Camp officials recounted having been able to hear the unfortunate man's screams for help, and later screams to his god to let him die. The sounds of bones crunching and splintering in powerful teeth came back to the terrified ears of everyone in camp who had huddled together for reassurance in the darkness.

Helpless to do anything since the government prohibited them from owning guns, there was nothing to do but listen to the sounds of agony coming less than a 100 yards from the edge of the clearing. It took quite a long time for the man to die, as the lion apparently began eating him from the foot upwards. And no matter what the Disney worshipers in this country try to tell you and your kids about wild animals, that's one hell of a way to die from a totally unprovoked attack. If you listen to the few quasi-celebrity individuals in this country who use their status to spread their opinions about animals (and fish, in the case of Jacques Cousteau), the lion had every *right* to convert a living human body into tablefare and later into fertilizer on the African plains. But just for the record, that one had not been raised from a baby in captivity and wouldn't answer to the name of Gentle Leo.

We had breakfast in the large Gathering Hut: fresh fruits, cereal, eggs, and fried bacon that was more lean than fat. Then we walked the path to the boat ramp and pier, loaded our gear and motored through the narrow cut ditch out onto the lake. The wind had died. The sun made me reach for a second coating of sunscreen even at 6:30 a.m.

Lake Kariba in western Zimbabwe is a huge lake with deep, rushing channels and vast expanses of shallow flats. We hoped to catch a few tiger fish for sport, and take several of the huge African bream for supper. The water was surprisingly clear, and already shimmering in the morning heat. Tiger fishing was unsuccessful for the first two hours, so we switched tackle and tried for bream. That was much easier. The bottom of the lake was basically bare throughout, except for patches of heavy vegetation growing at random around standing trees here and there, and quite easily spotted by easing the boat from one place to another while looking down into the water. Heavy-bossed Cape Buffalo gave us a malicious eye from the bank as we fished.

Our catch was not spectacular by standards of local fishermen who pay upwards of one dollar for a single fishhook in the Communist-run, economically crippled country which American politicos are trying to sanction South Africa into duplicating. My largest bream weighed about five pounds, a nice fight on light line.

Because of the ease in finding fish by merely looking into the clear water to locate patches of weeds, we caught almost 50 bream before quitting and returning to the shade, cool drinks and lawn chairs waiting back at camp. It was the only lake I have ever fished in a boat where depthfinders weren't needed.

Buck Taylor

Special Acknowledgements

The author wishes to express his thanks and appreciation to the following individuals who contributed, in a variety of ways, to the research and production of this book:

Dave Church & Jack Phillips
SI-TEX MARINE ELECTRONICS, INC.
Clearwater, Florida

Larry Colombo
TECHSONIC INDUSTRIES, INC.
Eufaula, Alabama

Thayne Smith
LOWRANCE ELECTRONICS, INC.
Tulsa, Oklahoma

Daniel Boone
GRAPHICS, INC.
Nashville, Tennessee

John Toft
Zimbabwe, Africa

Rick Clunn, Randy Fite, Johnny Morris,
Ray Scott

Mom, Dad, Harold and Claire

Bill, Doug, Teddy and Theresa

Fishing Success
with
Liquid Crystal
Depthfinders

1
Push-Button Efficiency?

Those of us who have watched the growth and advancements made by American sonar manufacturers in the last decade have observed a distinct trend towards making depthfinders "user friendly". The Computer Age invaded fishing several years ago, and the products marketed for finding fish in the water have become so sophisticated one only needs to turn the machine on and watch (or listen). Fish, structure and bottom are instantly recorded and displayed on the screen as your boat moves along. You can buy a unit which displays the fish in one color and the rest of the underwater world in another. You can buy units which scan the water around you and allow you to zero in on a single fish anywhere off to the side of the boat. And you can spend big bucks getting the latest models with all the gingerbread, or considerably less money buying perfectly workable machines that don't give you the time of day in Zurich. The choices are exhaustive.

17

Expertise with sonar comes only with practice and experience.
Today's LCD units make it much easier.

With the entrance of liquid crystal display units
(LCD) on the market, depthfinders took a giant step
towards the ultimate in ease of operation. If a chap can
find and punch the "Off-On" button on one of these
computer-driven machines, he can relax and watch the
show for the rest of the day on the lake without having to
touch it again. The automatic functioning of the unit in
changing power to adjust for different depths encountered will allow "hands off" operation, and the machine
will constantly be providing accurate, detailed information. Because of this, plus the present degree of detail
available, LCD depthfinders have stormed the market

and are enjoying huge popularity among fishermen and boat owners.

Basically, liquid crystal is merely a liquid in crystalline form, trapped between two pieces of polarized glass. When an electrical charge is applied from one side to the other, it causes the crystalline particles to "stand up," or align themselves in a perpendicular position like poles of a magnet. There is a reflector built into the unit behind the glass, and it reflects, or bounces back the light which enters from any outside source. The brighter the light, the stronger the reflection comes back out.

Crystal has a long, thin molecular structure. When electricity is used to align the particles in a perpendicular fashion, they interact with the polarized glass and block the return of reflected light on that particular spot of the screen. When the outside light is prevented from being reflected back out to your eye, the screen turns black by contrast. The entire screen is made up of small squares, or pixels, and each of them can be made to turn black by sending a charge to its location when returning signals are received from the transducer indicating fish, bottom or structure below. The liquid crystal in each of the other pixels on the screen which have not been electrically charged will be arranged in random fashion, allowing all the light to be reflected, thus appearing white in the absence of the blocking effect created in specific squares. The brighter the outside light, the better the contrast.

One variation of the conventional LCD screen mechanics is called "SuperTwist." Units sporting this

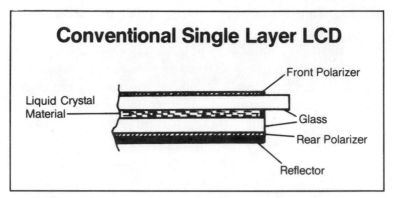

Basics of how LCD works. Courtesy Techsonic Industries, Inc.

feature are constructed to give a wider viewing area of the screen by adjusting each pixel to reflect light back at an angle greater than the normal 90-degrees. This allows the screen detail to be viewed clearly without having to sit directly in front of the unit. It also provides somewhat greater contrast, especially when coupled with tinted background reflectors. Another variation often associated with SuperTwist circuitry is the presence of a lighted background to further enhance detail.

Microprocessor circuitry routinely produces Space Age technology at your fingertips. You can examine a "slice," or layer of water at a time, or zoom in detail for a closer look at whatever catches your eye on the screen. There are noise reject features built into the better units which block out electrical interference and/ or eliminate "cross talk" between two or more different depthfinders running in the same boat. Quality units can eliminate most of the surface clutter by varying the sensitivity level in the receiver for close (surface) signals and more distant ones (fish and bottom).

Purely digital units are not discussed in this book. They're great for navigation and getting a true bottom depth reading. The better ones are guaranteed not to find fish.

Properly installed and operated, good depthfinders provide a staggering amount of useful information to the person who takes the time and effort required in learning how to read and interpret the signals. There are some requirements for study before becoming an expert with sonar but thanks to the simplicity of LCD, the time needed has been greatly reduced. You will find everything you need to know in this book, and you'll be using your unit like a pro in short order. Liquid crystal machines are infinitely easier to read and understand than the old flashers and paper graphs, but they still don't create hunger pangs in fish; neither do they cause fish to gather in mass beneath your boat. You have to search for fish and structure. And you have to understand what the unit is telling you.

Advances in sonar technology come faster than commercials on a midday TV show. Before I finish writing the next chapter, one or more electronic wizards will have gone to his or her boss with a spanking new idea on how to produce still another "advancement" in depthfinders. Before you finish reading this book, one or more of those ideas will probably be on the market, too.

It's comforting to realize no matter how many new bells and whistles they keep adding to depthfind-

*Finding productive structure out in open water becomes easy
once you master operation and interpretation.*

ers, the basic principles for operating them effectively
will remain rather constant. It actually doesn't matter
whether you see fish, structure and bottom signals on a
paper graph, a flashing neon bulb, a series of black dots
on a screen, or in a mass of different colors in video. The
basics of interpreting signals and getting the maximum
use from your machine are going to be pretty much the
same. For example, liquid crystal units don't tell you
any more than the paper graphs did, they just make life
under the boat easier to understand.

I don't favor one brand unit over another in this
material. The industry standards have reached such a
high degree of sophistication today that you can use

price and reputation as a reliable yardstick in making a purchase. Probably the only possible problem you should look at is the availability of quick, accurate repair service.

Your new LCD unit will give you many years of trouble-free service, and will provide meaningful data for you to use in applying your fishing skills and knowledge. Now that the engineers have discovered a way to eliminate most of the "clutter" and mysterious little signals which were confusing to the average guy on the water, you can concentrate on looking at fish and structure detail beneath the boat. Most of the fancy dancing you could do on paper machines can be duplicated by using some of the special features on LCDs today. But you can enjoy good, accurate information for fishing when simply running your LCD in the fully automatic mode, too.

Next, I presume the sonar manufacturers will come out with a trim little blonde cube which talks to you in a husky voice and serves cocktails every day at 5:00 p.m. Don't laugh; they have talking cars now, don't they? Anything seems possible in the Wonderful World of Depthfinders.

Push-button efficiency is available for fishermen today. Liquid crystal depthfinders made it possible. Now let's learn how to use them.

2

Transducers: The Weakest Link

Before you can do all the fancy footwork on the water with your depthfinder, the transducer must be properly installed. *Properly installed* is the key phrase, and it simply cannot be overly emphasized. No depthfinder can perform to its maximum ability unless it gets good signals from the transducer. Poor installation of the transducer is like putting old, rotten line on your fine new rod and reel. When you get into the fish, the frustration really begins.

I realize it's not much fun standing on your head trying to cement a little puck into an area of the boat where even a small monkey would get severe claustrophobia. Neither is it a pleasure kneeling on the gravel in your driveway while trying to drill straight holes through the transom so you can bolt on a semi-adjustable bracket of some sort. And since the boat obviously sits on the trailer at a different angle than it

Proper installation of your transducer is indeed the key to
getting maximum detail from your LCD.
Follow the instructions carefully.

will ride in the water when loaded, how many guys can duplicate a six-degree angle for the face of the transducer? There's also the very important question regarding the optimum location for the transducer to get best results. A difference of one or two inches in either direction could greatly affect your readout on some boats. Understanding how transducers work can be of real help in doing the installation later.

All transducers work basically the same, regardless of brand name, and regardless of whether designed for a chart recorder, flasher, or LCD unit. The depthfinder itself transmits precisely timed electrical pulses to the transducer which reacts by converting those electrical pulses into mechanical pulses of ultrasonic sound waves. The sound waves exiting the transducer leave in an imaginary cone shape, expanding in area as they travel downward. Technically, the sound area is shaped more like an oval-shaped balloon with "love handles," instead of an ice cream cone, but that makes little difference from a practical standpoint.

The sound waves travel through the water until they strike something and bounce, or reflect, off its surface. The reflected sound waves move through the water as an "echo" of the original pulse, and are received back by the transducer which dutifully sends the returning pulses on to the main unit. Based upon the time required for a pulse to leave the unit and be received back again, the distance the pulse traveled can be calculated and displayed on the screen to show the correct depth of the object below. Sound travels at about 4,800 feet per second in water, and the precise timing of

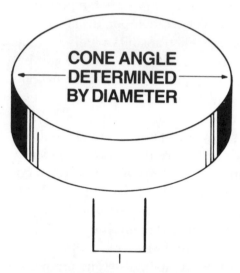

TRANSDUCER CRYSTAL

CONE ANGLE DETERMINED BY DIAMETER

FREQUENCY DETERMINED BY THICKNESS

The formula is a lot more complicated than this, but sonar manufacturers offer many different types of transducers based upon how they construct the man-made crystal within. Courtesy Techsonic Industries, Inc.

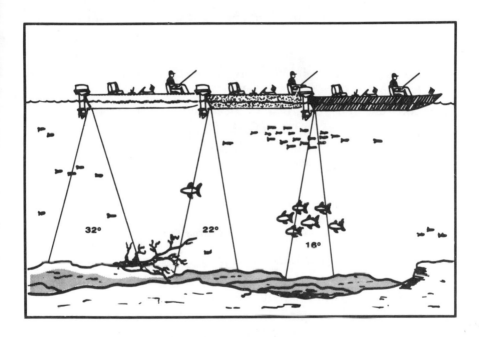

By changing the diameter of the transducer crystal, the cone angle can be made wider or more narrow.

the initial pulses, coupled with the time delay in receiving back an echo, allow very accurate readings of the distance between your transducer and the object below.

The bottom mass reflects constant signals and is displayed in a large, solid mass on the screen as you move along. Fish are inside the sound cone for only a short time, and they appear as individual readings suspended somewhere between the surface and bottom. If you stop the boat directly over a fish in the water, it will read as a solid line across the screen just like the bottom because the signal the fish reflects is remaining constant and being displayed as such. This all works fine until you introduce the problem of air bubbles.

Transducers refuse to work properly when surrounded by air bubbles. They cannot shoot signals through air or air bubbles in the water. Turbulence caused by having an irregular hull surface will create bubbles. Mini-keels and rivet heads cause such turbulence. If you have anything less than a perfectly smooth bridge between the transducer and the bottom of the transom, water rushing over the gap will create real problems in readout. Locating the transducer too close to the big engine can screw up the readings due to prop wash or cavitation. Even mounting the transducer inside the boat by cementing it to the floor can be bad if you get air bubbles trapped in the cement! And if your boat has a floor or double hull, you'll have to chop your way down to the bare skin of the hull before mounting the puck for best readings. Enough about the evils of air bubbles. Be sure you eliminate them.

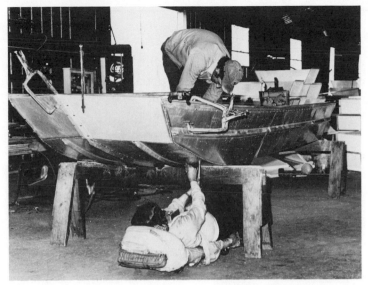

Aluminum hulls often create excessive water turbulence passing over the transducer due to rivets, welds, keels and even the drain hole for the livewell.

Transducers come in a variety of cone angles and frequencies. These differences are determined by the width and thickness of the transducer, and the formula is rather complicated. Each type transducer has its advantages and disadvantages under various conditions. Generally speaking, a medium cone angle with a high frequency is best suited to typical freshwater fishing situations. The wider-angle and lower-frequency transducers are ideal for the real deep water, especially the salty variety.

Depthfinder frequency is expressed in kilohertz (kHz), which is the frequency of the transmitter signal

Sounds simple, but the question "How much bottom area does my transducer cover for me?" is actually rather complicated to calculate. In fact, the amount of area being read by the unit can vary with the amount of sensitivity being provided, and even vary between different types of units (flasher, graph, LCD) using the same transducer! The chart below represents approximate area covered by different transducer cone angles on liquid crystal units, and was generated by the engineers at Humminbird:

Water Depth in feet	Diameter of area covered on bottom			
	16° cone	32° cone	36° cone	43° cone
10	3	7	8	10
20	6	13	16	19
30	8	21	26	31
40	11	28	35	41
50	14	35	43	52
60	17	41	51	60

through water. "Kilo" equals 1,000. "Hertz" describes the number of cycles per second. One hertz would be one cycle per second. Fifty kilohertz would be 50,000 cycles per second, and so forth. The higher the frequency, the more of the signal which gets lost, or absorbed, in the water, especially muddy and/or salty water filled with suspended particles. The lower the frequency, the further the signal penetrates the water without noticeable loss of detail.

A very popular frequency for freshwater application is in the 200 kHz range. The increased frequency provides exceptional detail on the screen, and the vast majority of freshwater fishermen have no need whatever to examine detail at 100-foot depths or better. The old salts who use sonar for finding shipwrecks and red snapper prefer a much lower frequency to provide the needed detail in the salty deep. Some manufacturers offer depthfinders with frequencies around 100 kHz, a nice compromise for either situation.

When you consider which frequency best suits your personal fishing requirements, you must also consider the cone angle of your transducer. Using the same frequency, a narrow cone angle will provide better deepwater performance than a wide-angle transducer. The narrow cone angle seems to concentrate the signals into a smaller area, thus penetrating better into the deep stuff. The manufacturers know all this, and they match cone angles to frequency to give optimum performance. But *you* must know what you're getting in order to use your machine most effectively under your own circumstances.

Narrow cone angles concentrate energy and give excellent readout in their limited circle of effectiveness. In addition, they don't confuse the issue by showing you everything within a huge area around the boat. They are great for navigation where you mainly want to see detail below the boat, and they make it easier to pinpoint targets when fishing, too. The wider cone angles are best when searching for fish or structure because they make it easier to find. But you have to sacrifice some knowledge of the exact underwater location of your target, as the cone area is so large the fish or drop-off you see could be 20 feet off to the side instead of right under your tennis shoes.

The angle and frequency of your transducer is a matter of personal choice, and should be considered carefully before making a purchase. Most depthfinders today can use any of several cone angle transducers, but you can't mix frequencies.

Mounting Procedures and Options

Probably the most common place to mount a transducer is hanging off the transom in the water. It's easier to do, and if the thing isn't exactly right afterwards, you can move it around a bit. Practically all the larger manufacturers today provide a rather detailed guide on mounting procedure, so I'll not go into all that. But there are some important practical considerations which usually aren't included in the instructions.

Boat hulls, like pretty women, come with a variety of shapes. The transducer must be positioned in such manner as to shoot its signals down under the boat and not off to the side unless you want to see what's under somebody else's boat on the lake. If the hull at the transom is slightly angled, such as a six-degree V found on many models, it's OK to mount the transducer flush with the edge and realize you are getting a very minor distortion off to one side. Nothing to worry about. Be sure the inner edge of the transducer side is pointing down, however. If the slope of the hull doesn't allow

Use sonar to catch fish in open water where
hidden structure lays.

that, you'll need to use a fairing block to reduce turbulence, or mount the transducer inside.

Be very sure the forward edge of the transducer is flush with the bottom of the transom to prevent air bubbles and churning water there. Build a small bridge with silicone if necessary due to a cheap bracket from the manufacturer. Be sure to smooth out the silicone completely.

Locate the transducer on the transom by taking your boat to the lake, running it at a variety of speeds, and physically observing the water flow under the transom. This is accomplished by having someone else drive the boat while you cautiously peer over the transom laying flat on the deck wearing a life jacket. Look for the smooth spot in the water where nothing on the hull configuration is causing air turbulence to exist beneath the transom. Mark the spot with tape or pencil, and return home or to the ramp to mount the transducer right there.

Once the bracket is secured and the transducer positioned, take the boat out for another spin and check the readout on your screen. If you're getting gaps in the bottom pixels, you're getting air bubbles across the transducer. Frequently, this can be eliminated by loosening the bolt and adjusting the face of the transducer to give more or less slant or "angle of attack" in the water. The heel or trailing edge of the transducer should be slightly lower in the water than the leading edge which is flush with the transom.

There are a couple of transducer brackets on the market today which are designed to place the puck well beneath the surface of the water, too. These are ideal for aluminum boats which typically generate excessive hull turbulence anyway. The good ones have a "kick up" spring in case you strike something in the water, and this could be the answer to eliminating air bubble problems on your boat if all else fails.

Another popular method for mounting a transducer is by cementing it to the hull inside the boat near the transom. The same procedure for locating the best spot is advised; look over the transom while underway to find the smoothest water area. Next go to a spot on the water where you know there is a drop-off. Anchor

Attaching the trolling motor transducer to a flexible rubber suction cup before mounting will allow the transducer to "give" slightly if contact is made with an underwater object, thus protecting the crystal from damage.

the boat directly over it. Hold the transducer overboard in your fingers and check out how the detail looks on your screen. Then place the puck on the spot you selected for mounting it on the inside of the hull. If there is a big difference between the two readouts, you have to find another place to cement the transducer to lessen signal loss. If the two readings are similar, mark the spot on the hull and return to the house.

You must sand down the floor or sump area for mounting until you get to raw fiberglass. Remove any dust and dirt. Be sure the boat is sitting level on the trailer. Use two-part epoxy cement, not silicone. Silicone has the tendency to remain as a gel beneath the puck, and can be affected by oil and gas spills later. Use slow-curing epoxy, not the fast-drying flavor. The speedy cements generate heat when drying, and that can generate air bubbles. Coat the face of the transducer with epoxy and set it aside. Pour the rest of the mixture onto the location and use a hair dryer for *only a few seconds* to warm the cement and further eliminate air bubbles. Place the pod into position and press down firmly. Work it gently to push out any trapped air. Put a weight on top of the transducer to hold it down and leave it alone for several hours. Don't let the kids play in the boat while the cement is drying.

One of the easiest and most handy places to mount a second transducer is on the foot of your trolling motor. You can employ a second depthfinder for it, or use a combo switch to run your unit from either transducer. A large hose clamp will secure the transducer to the body of the trolling motor, and the cord is carefully run up the

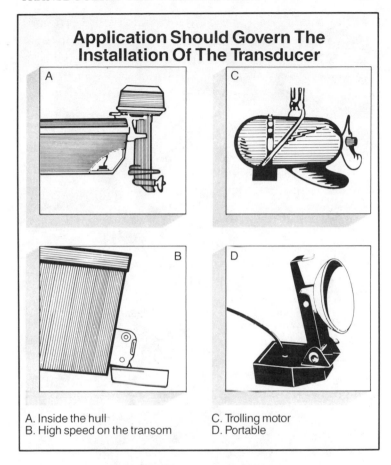

Application Should Govern The Installation Of The Transducer

A. Inside the hull
B. High speed on the transom

C. Trolling motor
D. Portable

Courtesy Techsonic Industries, Inc.

shaft out of harm's way when the motor is moved in and out. Use plastic thread-on ties to secure the cord to the shaft. You'll find a second unit up front is extremely helpful when fishing. If you prefer, a swivel mount can

*Transducers should be washed regularly with warm, soapy
water to insure there is no build-up of oil and grease on them
which reduces efficiency to perform.*

be used on your solo depthfinder, and with the combo switch you can get readings from the trolling motor transducer as needed. Happily, air bubbles aren't a factor for mounting the transducer on the trolling motor unless you run it in reverse a lot.

I can't close out this section without a few words on transducer maintenance. The things have a man-made crystal inside, and a sharp blow can ruin them. You would do well to keep the transducer away from both rocks and hard places. One common reason for transducer failure comes from parking your boat in a busy marina where the water is coated with oil and gas spills. Transducers can become totally "blinded" if allowed to absorb excessive quantities of petroleum products. *Regular* washing with warm soapy water will prevent the ailment.

Properly installed and maintained transducers will allow you to get the maximum benefit from your LCD. There's little or no maintenance required on liquid crystal depthfinders today, but your transducer still has to be pampered. It's the weakest link between you and successful readout.

3

Mounting The Unit: Where And How Many?

Having completed the critical chore of installing the transducer(s) properly, you're ready to mount the depthfinder itself somewhere in the boat. There are several choices for efficient location, but a few considerations on how you'll be using the unit when fishing should be looked at first.

The most typical spot for bolting down a depthfinder is on the steering console of the boat. This allows one to read the screen while motoring along searching for fish or structure. Before you start drilling holes, however, check for adequate clearance all around where the unit will be mounted. If you have a windshield on the console, be sure the unit won't be jammed in next to it so the plugs and cords get bent or worn bare with boat vibration. It's nice to be able to turn the angle of the depthfinder somewhat, too. Especially when your fishing pal wants to see what's going on under the boat

43

*Location of the unit(s) on the console must be done carefully
to insure maximum ease of viewing and operation
when underway.*

and you don't want him sitting in your lap to see the screen.

Don't get the unit too close to the steering wheel, either. Otherwise you'll be barking your knuckles on it every time you make a hard turn, and have trouble fiddling with the knobs and buttons when you want to use some of the special features. Finally, take a seat behind the wheel and have someone hold the unit down on your chosen location. Make sure you can see the full face of the unit clearly. Some boat manufacturers design their steering consoles more for cosmetics than efficient depthfinder mounting. If the surface angle is too steep, you won't be able to see the whole unit without standing up or sitting on a milk pail. I've had a couple of rigs where it was necessary to bolt a 2x8 board on top of the console to raise the mounting bracket enough to see the unit easily. It also allowed me to raise the power and transducer cords sufficiently to lift the lid on my beer cooler immediately in front of the console!

The mechanics of mounting the unit are simple enough. Today's LCDs have no moving parts to worry about, so they don't have to be pampered like the old paper graphs. A little bouncing around won't hurt much. It won't help, but won't do serious damage. Bolt the bracket securely in place after you've routed the cords where you want them under the console. The unit slips easily into the bracket and that part of the job is finished.

Swivel brackets are optional, and they are an advantage under some situations. They are essential if you decide to mount a second transducer up front on the trolling motor foot and use a power switch to change readings from one to the other. You could purchase an extra power cord and bracket to be used with the front transducer, then physically move the depthfinder up front when desired. It's a bit more effort that way, but works fine. Purchasing a second unit for the bow is probably the best possible solution, if your wallet can handle it.

The power cord and transducer cord which plug into your unit can be as finicky as a rich bride. At times they seem to function perfectly even in close proximity to other wiring in the boat. Sometimes they will pick up even the smallest amount of static from other sources. The best time to eliminate possible problems is during the initial installation of the cords. Many LCD units have built-in filters to eliminate outside interference, but there's no point testing them just for the heck of it.

In my opinion, it's keenly important you wire the depthfinder power cord directly to the main battery which fires the big engine in your boat. A lot of guys will wire them into a spare jack under the dash, but I'm still convinced there's no point taking a chance on picking up interference or losing power through the added connection. The boat builder could have used a different size wire, or have the circuits teamed up to use common fields when you run other accessories simultaneously with the depthfinder. Why gamble? Most LCDs come with long enough power cords to reach from the console to the battery anyhow. Spend another 75¢ and tape the power cord out of your way and away from the other wiring in the boat.

Find the channel in shallow lakes for outstanding action.

It can be a challenge trying to route the power and transducer cords from your unit to their intended locations in such a manner they don't rub elbows with any of the other wiring in the boat. This is especially true in the big bass boats where one opens the rear deck lid and sees enough wires to confuse the local utility company repairmen. Tape all that mess together in groups the best you can to allow some free space for the power cord. Use a small in-line fuse breaker on the positive wire from your depthfinder to the battery. A four-amp fuse should be about right. Then connect the power cords to the battery terminals securely.

Run the transducer cord along a path which will keep it the maximum distance away from all other boat wiring, especially those in the electrical system of your engine and tachometer. Flexible metal conduit, plastic hose pipe or liberal layers of plastic tape wrapped around the cord will all help shield the transducer cord from unwanted interference.

Be sure none of the wires you are installing will be rubbing against a sharp edge in the boat, and pay particular attention to the edges of the hole you drilled in the console. This is especially important on aluminum boats where the metal edge can quickly cut through the wires with only a minimum of time. Some depthfinder companies provide rings or clamps for use in securing the wires to the surface where you drilled the hole. Use them, or if unavailable, at least file and then tape the edges carefully.

If you decide to mount a second LCD in the bow of the boat, it's likely the factory power cord won't reach all the way back to the battery in the stern. This presents no problem, as the power cord wires can be extended by joining and soldering them with #12 or #14 automotive primary wire. Use a rosin-core solder, not the acid-core variety.

According to the experts, the exact type power supplied to your depthfinder is not critical. Almost all depthfinders today work on 12-volt DC current, and the differences between wet-cell batteries and those with dry cells have little or no effect upon performance. The wet-cell variety usually lasts a little longer in practice, but depthfinders are designed to use only the correct amount of current required. You will not get more or less power to the unit by using either wet or dry-cell batteries. In fact, you can operate your machine perfectly well by taking a pair of six-volt lantern batteries and wiring them in series.

Due to the mechanics of LCD units in blocking reflected light through the polarized sheets of glass, you may find one particular viewing angle slightly better than another. Before making a final decision on bolting the bracket on the console or front deck, do a bit of experimenting with positions and angles first. An adjustable mounting bracket can be a very helpful accessory here. Additionally, if you wear polarized sunglasses on the water, you may discover a "rainbow" effect with the light reflected off the screen since the unit is wearing similar glass. Usually a slight tilting of the screen will reduce the problem.

Before moving on to the next phase, I'll repeat my feelings on wiring your depthfinder power cord directly

*A second unit up front makes it much easier to stay over the
desired structure below once you have found it.*

to the main battery in the boat and not the one(s) which run the trolling motor. Your big engine constantly recharges its battery while running, providing a steady voltage level. If operated from the trolling motor battery, current to the depthfinder will get weaker and weaker as the day progresses. The *depthfinder* will not weaken the battery materially in a month of use. But the trolling motor will do it routinely in a matter of hours.

Depthfinders draw very little current from the battery, but they need their juice at full strength to operate at maximum performance levels. When a battery begins to weaken, it cannot provide a full dose of energy to the depthfinder, and the results suffer. You might compare the situation to having an all-night date with Dolly Parton after spending the afternoon with the three Mandrell sisters.

4

Features And Their Application

Because LCD units come in so many flavors and degrees of sophistication, it's not practical to spend the next 50 pages describing every single feature available if you bought one of each brand. There are new features being added to the line weekly anyhow, so the task would be almost impossible. However, there are several basic features on liquid crystal units which can serve a useful purpose under some conditions, and these will be discussed.

Zoom. One of the most frequently used features on LCD units, the Zoom allows one to expand the size of the detail on the screen at any given depth between surface and bottom. Normally, a set of dots or bars will act like a cursor on the screen, indicating the layer, or "slice" of water you are examining more closely. Some units can actually offer *additional* detail for you when you use the zoom on a particular segment of water,

Proper use of your LCD can generate success like this.

others merely enlarge existing detail for easier viewing. You shift the zoom range or layer depth to match the detail you wish to see, and punch a button typically marked "ZOOM". The enlargement appears instantly. On some units which sport the ability to update the entire screen of detail with every depth change, you'll notice a drastic change in the appearance of detail. You may wish to turn the zoom on and off several times over the same structure, just to get the hang of how the detail looks when zoomed onto the screen. Otherwise, things can look out of perspective momentarily after activating the feature. With the better units, you can change depth range while the zoom in activated, taking a closer look at each layer of water in sequence. With the total screen update ability, this would be similar to using a nice magnifying glass to enjoy a *Playboy* centerfold from head to toe, pausing on the "good parts" whenever you wish.

A common benefit gained with the zoom feature is your ability to more clearly separate fish from structure. Often fish will hold very close to the bottom, or next to treetops, etc. Their signals on the screen might be touching the structure itself, even though they obviously are slightly separated from it. The zoom lets you see space between the two types of returning signals, thus demonstrating there is indeed a fish there.

Bottom Lock. This feature merely locks the zoom mechanics on the layer of water immediately above the bottom, and changes automatically as the bottom depth changes. If you're looking for a particular type structure, or working around drop-offs with stumps and/or ledges, you might find this feature useful. You don't have to constantly change the zoom cursor to maintain contact with the bottom as it rises and falls under the boat. Be sure you know the *width* of your zoom layer, so you are aware anything beyond that distance above bottom will not be shown. For example, if your zoom (and bottom lock layer) width is 10 feet, you will get expanded detail on whatever is up to ten feet off bottom. A suspended school of fish holding 12 feet off bottom would go unnoticed.

Sweep or Display Speed. This feature acts like the paper speed on a graph recorder. You can adjust the speed of the detail appearing on the screen by increasing/decreasing this function. Generally, the faster your boat is traveling, the faster you want the display speed set. Slow it down when trolling or running at idle speeds searching for fish.

Manual Mode. This is the *only* mode of use on many LCD units, but on the fancy ones which have fully automatic circuits as well, the Manual Mode button can be utilized under special situations. When your unit is basically all automatic under normal use, the machine is using only the correct amount of power/sensitivity to get an accurate bottom reading. It follows that most of the fish and structure between surface and bottom will also be displayed with sufficient power. Yet there are times when using the Manual Mode instead of Automatic will give you specific readout otherwise missed.

One example of this is when you are looking for the thermocline in the water, and the bottom happens to be rather hard. The unit will be content with reduced

*Even in fairly shallow lakes and rivers, LCD allows you to find
deep holes which normally produce the better fish.*

power, as that's all it needs to pick up the hard bottom, and it can easily miss the change in water density which we call the thermocline. If you're interested in seeing the depth of the thermocline, which you should be in summer months, and the bottom under the boat is relatively hard, you should switch to the Manual Mode and bump up the sensitivity.

On some units which have the automatic operation capacity, use of one or more of the other features cannot be done in the Manual Mode. You must study the operator's manual carefully to determine what you can, and cannot, do when your machine is running manually. If your unit doesn't have the automatic operation ability, all this really doesn't matter. You set and adjust all the sensitivity and depth scales yourself to suit your needs for information. But don't short yourself on sensitivity, as that's the biggest mistake you'll likely make with manual-only units.

Alarms. Many LCD units today have fish alarms, bottom alarms or both. These alarms consist of a beeper, buzzer or an irritating little whine which sounds off every time you pass over fish, semi-floating debris, or get into water more shallow than the pre-set depth. If your hearing is bad, you won't hear any of them. If the wind is up, you'll hear them half the time. And if you turn the feature off, you won't have to worry about the noise at all.

There are, of course, times when these alarms are quite beneficial. Set properly, the bottom alarm will tell you in advance of running aground, and you can avoid situations hazardous to the health of your prop.

Anchored or drifting, the fish alarm can alert you to a school of fish which is making a getaway under the transducer. Most of the time, however, if you keep an eye on the screen, the display will tell you these things in black and white.

White Line. This "special effects" feature allows you to see the actual bottom signals in only a single line of pixels, then either shading or deleting the next row or three below that. The result is a narrow bottom line on the screen, making it easier to distinguish signals from fish holding there with their bellies almost touching the ground.

While there are dozens of special features being built into the present line of units on the market, the above represent the most common, and perhaps the most useful in the long run. The average fisherman will be quite happy with results obtained by running his machine in the Automatic Mode 99-percent of the time, relying on the technical genius which went in to the production of the product to be most adequate.

It's often quite helpful to know the bottom texture under the boat. Some species prefer rocky or gravel areas, others seek cover in weed beds and underwater vegetation. And as most bass fishermen know, their quary frequents "edge" areas where either structure or bottom conditions meet. LCD units have the ability to show you the type bottom below, but you have to know what to look at on the screen.

With most liquid crystal machines, the entire screen is blacked out from the bottom reading downwards. This is true whether the unit has an automatic

Discovering a deep hole below a power-generating dam will
almost always provide better action. A wide variety of fish
species relate to them.

mode or not. However, many manual units also have a sensitivity indicator, and by playing with it, you can often get a second echo on the screen, depending upon the brand depthfinder you are using. A second echo is basically a false reading which appears at exactly twice the depth of the true bottom, and is caused by the returning sound waves hitting the water's surface, bouncing back to the bottom and being reflected back up to the transducer once again. If you can get a second echo on your screen, you're in business.

The method for discovering bottom texture is most easily seen on units which have the automatic feature, but are being run on Manual. The second echo pops up clearly when you give the unit enough sensitivity. Here's how it works: soft bottoms absorb a good deal of the initial signal, and the automatic mechanics of the unit boost the power instantly to compensate and continue giving a good reading. But when run in the manual mode, the soft bottom absorbs enough of the signal to make the second echo disappear, or at least weaken very noticeably. When you see the second echo fade or disappear, you can be certain you are over mud or vegetation. The opposite is true of rock, hard sand or gravel bottoms; the signal is reflected back very strongly, and the echo gets wider and/or darker.

Although a bit tougher to do, you can see the type bottom texture when running a LCD in the automatic mode, but only if the unit has sensitivity bars on the screen. Sensitivity bars are little hash marks somewhere on the screen which indicate the amount of power the unit is being fed. The more power being used, the

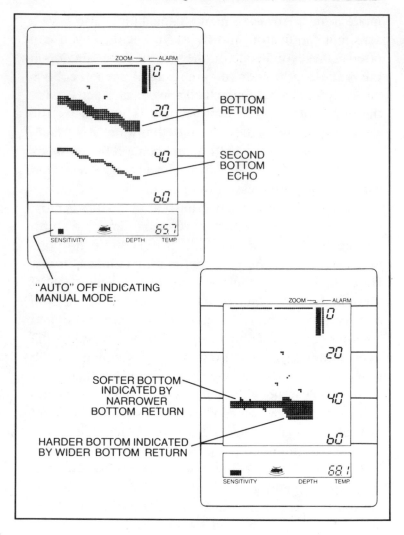

Using the Manual Mode, you can determine the bottom texture in two ways as shown above. Courtesy Techsonic Industries, Inc.

more little bars displayed out in the margin of the screen somewhere. Since soft bottoms require more power in the unit to be displayed properly, the sensitivity bars will increase materially when you pass over such areas. They will decrease when you go over hard bottom surfaces. By looking at the number of sensitivity bars on the screen, you can tell when the unit has automatically increased/decreased power to handle changing textures in the bottom below. Just remember soft bottoms get more attention than hard ones (no pun intended).

Any time you are running a LCD in the manual mode, each time you change to a deeper depth scale, you should bump up the sensitivity a bit. This provides the unit with sufficient juice to read and display small objects in the deeper area, things like structure and fish. Failure to increase the amount of sensitivity in the unit when you enter deeper water can result in the unit being unable to display some of the important details below. Train yourself to make a habit of doing this, and you'll get much better readout.

Most LCD units on the market today have some type of noise filter built into their circuits. They also may have a variable sensitivity control based upon distance away from the transducer. The advantages of these two internal mechanisms are important to the clarity of detail you get on the screen. The noise filter allows you to run more than one depthfinder in the boat at the same time, and prevents getting half-baked readings of what's under somebody else's boat when you get too close to it. It's one of the technical wonders available through modern electronic wizardry, as the unit can tell its own signals from those of any other, and will display only the signals it gives and receives. Should you have another depthfinder running in your boat which does not have this feature, it will go nuts when the signal cones overlap.

The variable sensitivity control also built into the better units acts as a surface clutter screen, eliminating most of the mess displayed in the first five or six feet of water below the surface. Air bubbles from your prop as you criss-crossed the area, heavy plant bloom and other minute objects in the surface layer of water often created a problem for depthfinder users, and it was almost impossible to tell if there was anything impor-tant in the first few feet of water as you went along. With the sensitivity control working to eliminate the tiny and unimportant signals close to the surface, you get a nice, clear and clean reading from top to bottom. Both the noise reject and sensitivity time control are features worth considering before making a purchase.

Most good LCD units have a control button or knob which can be used to adjust the speed at which the detail passes across the screen. This was mentioned briefly above under the feature "Sweep or Display Speed". It's worth mentioning again, as when you put it into practice, you'll find some pretty large differences in readout depending upon how you use the feature. One of the great advantages of LCD over the old flasher-type depthfinders is that the detail you pass over remains on the screen instead of disappearing almost instantly. It gives you time to study and react to what you see, and it

*Smallmouth prefer stair-step, rocky ledges, easily found
on sonar.*

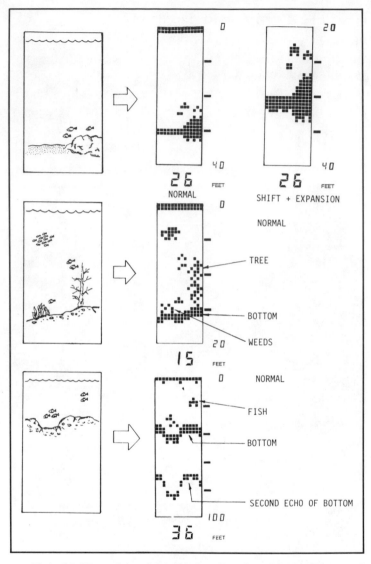

Typical LCD readout of detail below. Note how ZOOM feature in first example amplifies detail in selected layer of water. Courtesy SI-TEX Marine Electronics, Inc.

allows you time to interpret the signals better, too. As a result, the natural tendency is to run the screen display at a slow speed, retaining the detail for the maximum amount of time before it disappears off the edge. Unfortunately, a slow screen speed can cost you some important detail in the readout. As with a paper graph, running the boat along at trolling speed while looking for fish and structure, but keeping the screen (or paper) speed very slow, will compress the detail. You get only major images displayed, and they are all jammed together, making interpretation difficult.

If you increase the display speed, you spread out the detail on the screen, get better images of fish and structure, and generally see a lot more of the important detail below. You'll need to experiment quite a bit on the water, running the boat and unit at different speeds. But it won't take you long to figure out the optimum screen speed for different boat speeds.

Operating a depthfinder effectively comes with practice and time spent on the water. Some of the units on the market now come with built-in simulators, and those programs offer a genuine shortcut to efficiency never before available. I strongly suggest you use the simulator program, if your unit has one, to study and become familiar with how your machine operates. Take the unit into your living room and operate it with a couple of lantern batteries. Sit in the garage by your boat and run the LCD through its paces while you enjoy a cool drink and watch it rain outside. Play with every single button and knob on the unit while it's in the simulator mode, and watch carefully how the detail

changes. You probably can learn more about how your particular machine operates and reacts to manual changes with the buttons by spending an hour like that than you can learn in three or four days on the water.

Regardless of what the big color advertisements tell you, you're not going to become an expert with LCD overnight. Sorry folks, it takes time, study and experience. You will gain expertise in direct relation to the amount of time and effort you spend working, studying and experimenting with your depthfinder.

5

Successful Fishing With LCD

When you combine your operating skills of the unit with your knowledge of fish habits and habitat, you quickly begin to improve your catch. Outdoor writers have published a great deal of poop on how 10 percent of the fishermen catch 90 percent of the fish, etc. And you have heard statistics on how 90 percent of the fish are found in only 10 percent of the water area. Personally, I don't think all that stuff smacks of reality, but there obviously is some truth to the fact only selected anglers "in the know" about finding fish are going to be the guys who bring home filets on a regular basis.

A working knowledge of how to use your depth-finder will immediately place you in the "select" group of anglers who are supposed to be catching all the fish. One of the great things about sonar readout is that it tells you both positive and negative things about what's going on below your boat. When you see fish on the screen, you have no doubt about their location. But sonar also allows you to eliminate the unproductive water in the lake by displaying the *absence* of fish. There's no point working water where there are no fish, so you can begin searching at any given point in the lake and keep on moving until you hit the magic area where fish are waiting for your bait. Eliminating the fish-void water is just as important to success as finding the good places. Depthfinders are often called "fish finders". They also serve to show you the places where fishing is a waste of time.

The following pages are comprised of numerous actual fishing experiences on the water around the country where depthfinders played a serious role in my successful attempts to bring home tangible results for the suppertable. You will find tips, tactics and screw-ups I have encountered along the way in learning about fishing for several different species. From these, you should be able to learn some time-saving methods for increasing your own personal pleasure on the water. At least, that's the whole point in putting this particular chapter in the book.

It should be mentioned there is no substitute for spending time on the water with your unit(s). The advances of liquid crystal display machines have made possible the growth from beginner to semi-expert with sonar a very real, and rather quick, reality. In years past, it took one several years to make the transition. You will find your ability to read fish and structure signals on your LCD will come easily. And when you apply your personal knowledge of the type structure

Knowing how to find appropriate structure in open water will produce excellent action.

your favorite species of fish is most likely to be using at a given time of year, the combo will result in good stringers or winning weights at local tournaments.

Some of the stories following are condensed versions of articles I have sold to national magazines. Some are short, unique accounts of events where sonar was the key to my success. And each description of a fishing adventure is offered here to give you the advantage of learning rapidly about how to catch one or more of your favorite species without having to spend months or years in trial and error efforts. Fishing can be easy if you apply your knowledge, use the right equipment, and take full advantage of the information your LCD provides for you.

Bass

I thought the man was joking, but he looked me straight in the eye and stated he could tell if a bass would bite or not by the way it appeared on his depthfinder. The man was Randy Fite, and he was a true expert with depthfinders, but come on now, was I supposed to believe a claim like that, really?

The comment came during an interview with Fite in his hometown of Conroe, Texas. I had been sent there to do an article on bass fishing with Randy, and gather some tips on how he uses depthfinders to increase his success consistently. I was polite, but secretly couldn't swallow the idea he could look at a fish on the screen and tell if it would bite or not. I was wrong.

"Active" bass move into direct contact with the structure they are relating to, and this move can be seen easily on your display screen.

After the interview, Fite took me in his boat out onto Lake Conroe. It had been raining for several days before my arrival, and the water was high, muddy, and generally a mess.

"We'll have to hunt for them, Buck," Fite remarked. "Most of my favorite spots aren't going to be very productive in this high, muddy water."

Randy ran the boat upstream a couple of miles, then slowed the boat and turned on his depthfinder. A few minutes later, several fish appeared on the screen. I congratulated my host on finding them so quickly, but he shook his head.

"Those aren't active bass," he said factually. "Let's move on up and find some more."

He repeated the process twice more, much to my amazement each time he ignored the find and went hunting again. Finally, he found a bunch to his liking and pitched a marker buoy off to the side.

"These should do it," Randy said as we started fishing for them.

Both of us had a hook-up on the second cast. When the action slowed, Fite cranked the big engine again and we started hunting for more fish. Each time the man said we were going to catch fish, we did exactly that. It was almost spooky. But I couldn't help wonder about all those schools of fish we had passed up along the way.

I fished with Randy the next day also. This time he let me challenge his claim, although my ego would have been better off if he had not. I spent hours casting at schools of bass he said were "inactive", and caught a total of two fish. We caught five bass at the first stop where *he* wanted to fish.

Until it was proven to me rather forcefully, I seriously doubted Fite's statement that you could look at bass on a depthfinder screen and determine if they would bite or not. He made a believer of me that day in Conroe, and I have since proved it many times in my own boat.

There is a definite pattern to the way bass behave when they are feeding (active) and when they are suspended (inactive). The differences between the two types of behavior are easily seen on a good unit. They do act in a predictable fashion which you can use in catching more of them because of your LCD. Your ability to *see* how they look down there will do wonderful things for the weight of your stringer.

When a bass begins to feed, he approaches structure in the water. The structure is holding the menu upon which he is about to dine. He will actually come into physical contact with that structure in his efforts to gobble minnows and crayfish living there. Conversely, when the bass has his belly full and wants nothing more than to relax, daydream or rest peacefully, he pulls a short distance away from the structure and suspends. It's reasonable to assume you will catch more bass when they are hungry and feeding than you will by chunking hardware at them while they sit around dormant with a full tummy. How the bass relates physically to the structure tells you when those short periods of activity are about to fill your ice chest.

You can see when the bass come into contact with the structure simply by watching where the signals appear on the screen. When the fish signals on your unit are several feet away from the structure, the fish are going to be uncooperative at best. You can run to another part of the lake and hope the fish over there are following a different bus schedule. It is wise to continue checking back on the inactive school you have found from time to time. They gotta eat sooner or later.

Another tip-off about how feeding bass appear on your display comes from the way they school together. Inactive bass avoid conversation with others. But as bass begin to feed, they bunch much more tightly together. This is probably a bit of the old killer instinct in them. A wolf pack in the north woods bands together and uses teamwork to down a caribou. Bass probably have some of that same predator ingenuity when chasing stuff they like to eat.

Using a LCD, you can observe how bass relate to structure, and you can tell if they are going to bite readily or not. It's true. Interestingly enough, when water conditions get pretty lousy down deep, and the bass have to live several feet above the structure, it still works. They suspend off to one side above the structure they are relating to; when they begin to feed, they move directly over it.

———————————————————————————

Fall is one of my favorite times for bass fishing. You can find them in both shallow and deep water, and as a bonus, the larger bass are becoming active again after a long, lazy summer. Accurate use of depthfinders at this time of year can produce spectacular success by allowing you to concentrate your work in productive water.

*Open water bass fishing can generate outstanding success once
you master your LCD readout.*

Regarding shallow-water efforts, creek channels are prime places to fish. You might begin out at the mouth of the creek where water is about 10 to 12 feet deep on the shoulder of the channel, tapering down to perhaps 20 or 25 feet in the channel itself. Using your sonar to stay on course, begin working the channel banks systematically as you progress up the creek. Bass don't always hold right on the lip of the channel, but they stay pretty close during this period.

A lead spoon is quite effective for working out a creek channel. It gets to the bottom quickly and is easy to cast. Bounce it on the lip and let it fall into the channel. Make the lure "hop" a couple of times, then repeat the procedure. You can use the depthfinder to "crisscross" the channel with the boat, finding structure and staying in the productive area.

Creeks filled with brush might best be worked with shallow-running crankbaits. Run the lure just deep enough to clear the top of the brush. You are trying to locate the fish at this point, not fill the ice chest, so use a lure that works efficiently in the structure encountered. When you find those fish, then you can switch over to another more deliberate technique which may work better.

As you get further back into the creek, switch to a smaller size crankbait, worm, jig, etc. Usually, the bass found way back in the creek during fall will be smaller than those still out near the main lake where the water is deeper. If you have several below-freezing nights all of a sudden, as sometimes happens in fall, you may have to switch to a *real* tiny bait. Fast-dropping water tem-

Success goes hand-in-hand with depthfinder expertise.

*Even in hard winter conditions, you can use your LCD
and personal knowledge of bass habits to bring home
good stringers.*

peratures will clobber fish in shallow places. Their
metabolism will slow down to approximate a state of
shock, and it will take *very* small baits worked *very*
slowly to get them.

Another good spot for finding fall bass is a moss
bed, practically anywhere in the lake you can find one.
Bass love these things, and the action can be excellent at
almost any time of day. Here again, use the lure that

seems best suited for the initial encounter with the bass. Crankbaits would likely stay fouled most of the time; so would spoons. Spinner baits would be an ideal choice for use in searching for bass around moss beds. The plastic worm would work well, also, but would be pretty slow if you have a large area to cover.

Cover the moss bed completely. Work the lure all around the outside edges, over the top and in the middle where there are pockets. Bass could be holding practically anywhere in the structure. They *could* be just sitting off to one side admiring it.

Rock and rip-rap will hold a surprising number of bass in the fall months, too. The best method for fishing that type structure is to position your boat near the edge and cast up or down the shoreline, bringing the lure back parallel to it. Crankbaits or spinner baits produce well, worked from one to five feet away from the edge.

During an interview with bass fishing pro, Rick Clunn, he gave me some points to remember about fall bass fishing. Rick breaks down fall fishing into two parts: "early fall" and "late fall". This is due to the possible changes in the oxygen levels you find in so many lakes at this time of year. For example, the month of September can still be considered part of summer in some areas, and the lake may well have bad oxygen in the deep water areas. This puts more fish up shallow, obviously. In November, the oxygen usually is good back down to the 18-to-25-foot range, and many bass will move back out in the lake to deeper structure. Water temperatures have a lot to do with this, although Clunn doesn't pattern his fishing around water temperature. He patterns his fishing around a number of things, but one of the most important is what he sees on his depthfinders.

Your alternate choice for bass fishing in the fall is deep water, generally considered to be water between 15 and 30 feet. In this situation, the distinction between early and late season is even more critical. Oxygen levels can still be bad in most warm climate areas, causing fish out in the main lake to be suspended over structure instead of down around it. Suspended bass are usually harder to catch, and the vertical jigging technique which often works best is tough to master.

The plus side of deep water fall fishing comes from your ability to use your depthfinder to cover a great deal of water accurately without ever wetting a line. You never even have to cut off your boat's engine until after you have found fish. The procedure is to motor from one deep-water structure to the next, checking each spot for fish. If they are on the structure, you can see them with sonar. If not, you merely drive to the next place. There is no point fishing unproductive water, and once you have learned to read your depthfinder well, you can cover a sizeable chunk of the lake without wasting time.

You run to the structure, then check out the action with your screen. *Once you have gained the skills for finding active bass before you shut down the big engine on the boat, your fishing success in deep water will improve fantastically!*

Ideally, you might have a second depthfinder in the boat. This one would be in the bow, the transducer mounted on the trolling motor. Once active bass have been located, the trolling motor sonar unit allows you to stay directly on top of the fish. Vertical jigging requires accurate lure presentation for success.

Having never read any of today's fishing magazines, your depthfinder cannot tell the difference between a 15-inch bass and a 15-inch carp. It displays both equally on the face of your unit, so it becomes your job to tell the difference between bass and other species. But in the case of a single fish of moderate size, you won't know purely by looking at his picture on sonar. You have to use your knowledge of fish habitat to help figure it out. A single fish out in deep water away from structure will probably not be a bass.

Vertical fishing with a spoon, grub or plastic worm is quite effective. You must place the offering accurately in the productive zone where the fish are, and the difference can be only a matter of a yard or so in cold weather. If the fish show up on your unit at 20 feet below the surface, working your bait several feet above or below the school won't do much for your reputation as an expert. And many times, deep-water bass group together tightly, making it possible for the guy in the bow of the boat to get action with almost every drop, while the dude in the back never gets a hit!

Most strikes while vertical jigging, maybe 90 percent, will come as the lure drops or flutters downward. You can't afford to have slack in your line at that critical moment, so after you "hop" or pull the lure upwards, catch it there with your line. Then follow the lure back down by lowering your rod, keeping the line tight. If you establish a set rhythm for doing this, you'll notice instantly any variation in the way the line acts.

Author with ten-pounder taken from junction of creek and river channels in 15-foot water.

Even if you don't feel the fish strike, a twitch or slight pause in the line tells you a fish has hit, and you set the hook immediately.

Deep-water bass fishing is both fun and productive, although most people never try it seriously. Learn to use your depthfinders well and you'll find this method for taking bass is deadly.

With wooden paddles battered and chipped from years of dispatching Cottonmouths sunning themselves on logs and stumps, we threaded our way silently in the canoe through tall, standing cypress trees shrouded in Spanish moss. Mist rising from the water as the orange sun sent fingers of light between the trees generated a timeless, soul-stirring scene of total solitude. Neither Jerry nor I spoke as we dipped our paddles into the black water and stroked gently. The swamp was awakening with the movements of birds and squirrels greeting the day, and the subtle sounds of raccoons, bobcats, and owls retiring from the night shift.

Perhaps twenty minutes after we had shoved the canoe into the water at the edge of the swamp, we came upon a large opening in the trees shaped somewhat like the back leg of a cat. This was the little cypress lake where Jerry had been bass fishing for so many years, catching respectable numbers of good largemouth with shiners in summer, spinner baits and crankbaits in fall and spring. The surface of the open area displayed a zebra pattern of light and shadow as the sun barely cleared the horizon and its low angle pushed long, skinny rays through the mist and across the water between the trees.

Positive no man had ever done it before me, I turned on the little portable depthfinder and began exploring the most intimate secrets of this remote, primitive cypress lake. I almost felt guilty introducing Space Age technology into such surroundings. Almost immediately, the screen began displaying signals from numerous fish swimming below us. I felt far less guilty when we passed over a deep hole and the edge of it was literally covered with fish!

We marked the spot by trying to line up and remember a couple of leaning trees on both banks, then backed away quietly to the outer edge of our casting range. We rigged our lines and began casting to the edge of the drop-off.

"They could be crappie, by the way they're massed in there," I told my friend, breaking the silence. "I'll try a small jig and you run a crankbait past them, OK?"

Jerry caught a two-pound crappie on his crankbait with the second cast. I caught the underwater snag they were congregating around with my jig. At Jerry's suggestion, we turned on the depthfinder again and began searching for bass. We spent some 30 minutes examining the bottom all over the little lake. There were shelves, drops and a mysterious ditch out in the center. We found mossy flats and one particularly steep drop-off which was holding fish around the shoulder. And we caught bass easily after discovering those places. Jerry's success had come previously by working the edges of the lake with his lures and bait. He had no way

Larry Nixon handles nice bass in remote area.

of knowing about the structure out in the middle where the larger concentrations of fish were living.

We caught several dozen bass, releasing all but four for supper. Each time we wet our hands before unhooking a fish, Jerry expressed his amazement at our luck. In the years he had fished the lake, he had never experienced action like we were enjoying together. When he gently slid a fat, healthy nine-pounder back into the water, our largest of the day, Jerry just shook his head silently and watched the fish swim away.

Very few fishermen take advantage of the excellent fishing to be found in remote swamp ponds and lakes. For whatever reason, some bass anglers prefer taking their big rigs to the public waters of overfished large reservoirs and whiz around at full tilt all day looking for an elusive "honey hole". Gearing down to enjoy catching bass without screaming engines and expensive rigs eludes them. Maybe that's one reason so many small lakes in hard-to-reach places grow such outstanding populations of bass these days.

A little effort and a portable depthfinder can put you onto some of the best bass fishing you have ever encountered, if you're willing to experiment back off the worn track in many of the swamps and beaver ponds which cover countless acres of American topsoil. Using your knowledge of bass and their preferred habitat on structure, and having the structure displayed for you clearly on a portable sonar machine, will open new and wonderful areas to you in the more remote places others overlook. You can bet on it.

As Jerry and I paddled lazily back toward the

*Getting back into remote areas will typically produce
outstanding action on a variety of fish. It can be great fun.*

pickup parked on the edge of the swamp, we relaxed and counted our blessings amid pure fresh air, sights and sounds of the wild area, and total absence of any other humans. We knew we would be back. We didn't even tie gaudy ribbons on the trees to aid in marking our newly-discovered structure. The depthfinder could find it all again in a matter of minutes.

Crappie

Very few fish lend themselves to depthfinder use better than crappie. Their movements are predictable with a good degree of accuracy as they migrate back and forth in the lake, and sonar skills allow you to find their little wet noses with ease.

While it is self-evident that crappie move into the shore to spawn during springtime, the activity is not one which can be isolated to an exact date on the calendar. Many a vacation has been planned months in advance to coincide with the crappie spawning runs, only to discover the action was much better the week before. Or the week after.

During the spring, crappie can be rather unpredictable. This is due in part to the things which affect their daily life. Spring itself, is unpredictable in nature. When the weather breaks, presenting several gorgeous, warm days in a row, the females move into shallow water, preparing to lay their eggs. Then it rains. Or it turns cold and drops the temperature a bit. The females react by retreating into deeper water, playing a "wait-and-see" game. Presumably, this is equally frustrating to the male of the species.

In bodies of water which eventually flow through a man-made dam, spawning crappie are often influenced by the guy who controls the gates. They may move into the shallow water, find a housesite, and awake the next morning to find the gatekeeper has dropped the lake level several inches. Heavy spring rains often make gatekeepers do things like that. Again, the crappie must back off to reconsider.

Combinations and changes in water level and temperature make it practically impossible to pick the exact date and location for crappie to spawn. The spawning season usually will cover a four-to-six week period, with fish coming and going steadily like picnic ants hot on the trail of a Honey Bun. There can be little doubt of finding crappie near shore in springtime, but exactly *where* they are on a given day is not all that easy to guess. They can be almost anywhere in the general area of the creek mouths. Shallow, deep and suspended.

Depthfinders allow fishermen to locate the underwater structure which crappie like: drop-offs, creek channels, stick-ups, stumps, etc. While bank fishing for spawning crappie is by far the most-used technique, backing your boat out into the open water over this type structure can produce much more consistent success in the spring. For one thing, all crappie do not go to the bank for spawning at the same time. This is why the activity lasts for several weeks. New arrivals are moving in all the time. And they work that off-shore structure *both* coming to and going from the bank.

*Use your LCD to find drop-offs and structure out away from
shore. The results are often much better.*

Bank fishing may be unpredictable because of weather conditions, but catching crappie several yards away from shore on structure is a sure bet.

Many experts on crappie fishing are convinced the really *large* crappie spawn in eight to 12-foot water around stumps. Another reason to work away from the bank.

The most efficient tackle and technique for catching deeper-water crappie was demonstrated to me many years ago on Kentucky Lake. It consists of two hooks spaced about 18 inches apart, with a one or two-ounce lead weight attached to the line either between the hooks or an additional 18 inches below the bottom hook. With a lively minnow on each hook, the procedure is to "walk" or "bounce" the lead weight along bottom in the structure. You actually can "feel" the structure as the lead weight touches it while you concentrate on keeping a tight line.

Having two hooks spaced apart in this manner, you offer your bait at different levels simultaneously. Strangely, you find most of your fish will hit either one or the other. That small difference in depth can make a material difference. Of course, you catch two crappie at the same time on occasion. Thin wire hooks are used because the procedure naturally involves getting hung on the structure. With practice, you learn to raise and lower your pole gently when the rig gets hung on something. The lead weight usually will dislodge the tangled hook as it drops back downward. If this fails, you can pull straight up on the line, and the thin hooks will straighten out, releasing the structure.

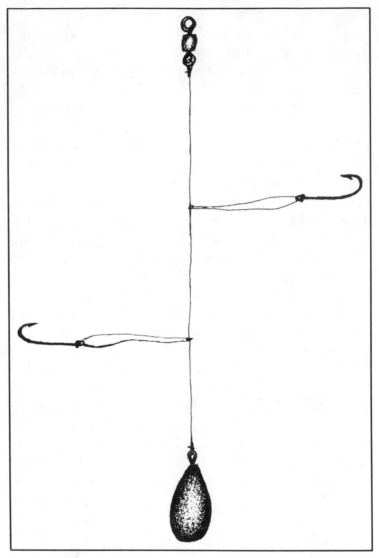

*Typical tightline or "bottom-bumping" rig used so effectively on
a wide variety of fish.*

Sensitive poles, usually between 10 and 15 feet in length, work best for the bottom-bumping method. You can purchase a fiberglass pole designed for this needed sensitivity, use a cane pole with a good tip, or convert your old fly rod into a crappie-catching tool. It helps greatly to have a line keeper on the pole. You can wrap excess line around the spool or cleat, using it later when you enter deeper water and the additional mono is needed to reach bottom.

Tight-line fishing, or "bottom bumping" is fantastically productive on crappie every month of the year. When you feel a fish tap the bait, set the hook immediately; don't wait for him to tote the lead weight off somewhere. I suggest you use at least 15-pound monofilament line for this technique. You'll need enough line strength to survive while straightening out the wire hooks which refuse to "jiggle" free of brush. And you may need it for landing a much larger fish that chomps your minnow down there. Tales of boating big bass and catfish on these crappie rigs are common.

Some professional crappie guides use 40-pound line for their double-hook rigs. They neither like to waste time on snags, nor spend the day tying on new terminal tackle for their customers. If the water you fish is on the cloudy side, you probably can use the heavy stuff O.K. But if your lake is fairly clear, you'll catch more fish by using line in the 15 to 20-pound class.

"I was afraid of this," one fisherman tells the other after several fruitless hours on the water. "Should have stayed home and weeded the garden."

Beautiful stringer of "slab" crappie located on deep drop-offs.

"Yeah. The spawn is definitely over and we're wasting time," his companion replies. "Wonder if the guy at the bait house will buy back these unused minnows?"

Unfortunately, that's a typical scene among crappie fishermen in summer months. The fish indeed have left the shallow shoreline structure after completing their annual spawning activities, and the vast majority of fishermen simply don't know where to find them. Crappie gear is put away for the remainder of the year, and fishermen turn their attention to other species in the lake. In so doing, they miss out on what is actually the easiest time of year to catch crappie in good numbers.

It's August. A family of four is vacationing in one of the little rental cabins on a public lake. The noon sun is baking that part of the world with wilting intensity. Mother and daughter are relaxing under the air conditioning like most others around the area. The man running the boat dock had been surprised when father and son rented a small craft, bought some minnows and headed straight for the middle of the lake. He, like the other guys around, thought the pair was just another inexperienced twosome wasting time in the summer heat.

With a small portable depthfinder clamped onto the bow, Dad eased the boat around out in the middle of the lake until they found the old river channel. Working along the shoulder of the channel, Dad looked for stumps, brush or little stair-step drop-offs on the shoulder. A couple of floating buoys were dropped over to mark such spots, and the two began fishing for crappie.

Wide-brimmed straw cowboy hats kept the direct sun off their heads. Suntan lotion covered their arms, legs and faces. Within two hours of fishing in the blistering August heat during the "worst" time of day, the father and son had put 37 nice crappie on ice in their Coleman chest. The resulting stir back at the boatdock when they returned with their catch was the only thing "typical" about their day.

"Sometimes we catch a lot more," the boy was heard telling someone in the crowd which gathered.

Those who know how can catch summer crappie under conditions most fishermen believe to be totally impossible. Actually, catching big stringers of crappie

*Crappie fishing can be a real fun outing in the hot months of
summer when others usually stay at home.*

in August is easier to do on a *consistent* basis than at any other time of year. It's a fact.

Crappie move around in the lake during the year, their actions rigidly controlled by water temperature. This makes them predictable. Water temperatures are constantly changing year-round, *except* in the dead heat of summer. The cold fronts are gone, the late spring flurries which cause spawning action to "stop and go" are gone. All is calm and stationary in the crappie's environment. So he is very easy to find and catch. More so than at any other time.

"Drop it!" I told my fishing partner who was holding one of the floating marker buoys. "That looks like the spot where the creek channel enters into the river. If so, we've just hit the jackpot!"

My pal Doug Sory and I were fishing a very large reservoir for the first time. It was late summer and by ten o'clock in the morning the temperature had already hit the 100-degree mark. Doug had been pretty skeptical about our chances of catching crappie, and had been rather vocal expressing his opinions. One of the nicer things he said was that I was crazy.

"Crappie follow migration routes in the lake much like many other species," I explained. "If this spot actually pinpoints where that little creek over there flows out and hits the main channel of the lake, we've found a crossroad in their movement routes, and there should be plenty of fish nearby. I can see brush down there with the depthfinder, too. Get your gear ready!"

We had tossed out four buoys along the channel edge, marking its route for some 100 yards with bobbing orange floats. I worked the trolling motor back towards

Sharp drop-offs, even close to shore, can be the key to catching good stringers of crappie in spring months.

shore slightly, trying to determine if we actually had found the creek channel intersection. Two more buoys were dropped shortly thereafter, and we had a clear picture of the scene below.

Doug only grunted when I said "We're gonna kill 'em today!"

As water temperatures begin to climb in early summer, crappie begin a migration back out into the main lake and deeper channels of the river. All crappie don't do this, as witnessed by the occasional one you'll snag back in the shaded cuts and more shallow areas near cool underwater springs. But the vast majority of crappie head straight for the old river channel where they find some relief from the heat in deeper haunts. You will almost always find the larger crappie there.

It was a banner day for crappie fishing, and it didn't take Doug long to admit it. We began picking up fish almost immediately, and put over 20 into the ice chest in the first hour. By two in the afternoon we had our limit of 35 crappie each, and headed for shore. It was just that easy, and the fun can be repeated day after day in July and August.

There are some tricks to catching hot-weather crappie which are important to know. You'll need a good depthfinder to find the old river channel out in the lake and spot brush on the shoulder. You'll need floating buoys to use in marking the drop-off, and you'll need a trolling motor or good arm for skulling the boat from buoy to buoy while fishing.

The most effective rig to use is what we call a "tightline" or "bottom-bumping" outfit. It consists of a heavy bell sinker tied to the tag end of heavy monofila-

The tightline rig can be made at home, or purchased at many baitshops. It works year-round for crappie fishing.

ment line. Eighteen inches above the sinker, a loop is tied in the mono and a 3/0 thin wire crappie hook is threaded onto the loop. A second hook is attached in the same manner another 18 inches above the first one. A foot above the top hook, a snap swivel is tied on, and used to attach the rig to your main line. Long fiberglass rods or poles are best suited for this type fishing. Flyrods will work in a pinch. The idea is to have a rod or pole which is lightweight and sensitive, yet long enough to allow easy raising and lowering of the rig.

This rig is often called a "bottom bumping" outfit because that's exactly how it is used. A pair of live minnows are placed on the hooks and the weight is allowed to sink to the bottom. Excess line is taken in until there is no slack, and the pole is lifted and lowered constantly to "walk" the sinker along the bottom as the boat eases over the area. It's essential you keep the line tight in order to feel the fish strike.

This method is deadly, and requires only minutes of practice to become efficient with it. Before long you will be able to "feel" the sinker strike underwater structure; it has a very different "thump" when striking a stump or just brushing the limbs of a sunken treetop. You can even tell the difference in the sinker hitting hard bottom versus soft mud or vegetation!

Use the trolling motor to slowly move the boat along the channel shoulder, walking, or bouncing, the pair of minnows along the bottom. If you find a particularly good clump of structure, drop over another buoy on the spot and keep coming back to it for repeat action. And once you have found the old river channel in hot weather, you'll literally have *miles* of good crappie fishing at your disposal.

Probably the best place to catch summer crappie is where the old river channel shoulder comes up from about 40 feet to maybe 12 feet on top. In July and August, crappie will be holding somewhere between the 30-foot to 10-foot level along that slope. You can bet on it. As a bonus, there will be several other species of fish in the same area. We often catch bass, bream, sauger and catfish while tightlining these areas for crappie. If you could look underwater, you would be amazed at the vast numbers of fish down there!

As you pass over drop-offs along the channel shoulder, let out sufficient line to keep the sinker in contact with the bottom. Some fishermen tape simple cleat-shaped line keepers onto their fiberglass poles for this. Others attach small spinning reels to the pole. You may have to experiment a bit on depth initially to find the productive level, but once found, you'll have a steady, action-filled day.

The purpose in having two hooks on the rig spaced 18 inches apart is not to catch two crappie at once, although this happens quite often. Crappie often suspend slightly off bottom, and there are days when you will catch most of your fish on the top hook and not the bottom. When you see this pattern exists, you can lift your pole slightly when around structure, placing both hooks into the productive zone.

Summer crappie are not as aggressive as spring crappie in taking the bait. Often they appear a bit on the lazy side, and when they take a minnow they do

*Larry Colombo with nice stringer of crappie taken on drop-offs
out away from shore.*

*Portable LCD on a canoe allowed these anglers to fish
the swamp.*

it gently. It's important you set the hook instantly whenever you feel a tap. The fish is not going to take the minnow and run off with it somewhere. And when you find a stump or treetop on the bottom, hold your bait there for several seconds before moving it away. There are occasional days when it's necessary to "tease" the crappie into biting. With the dual-hook rig, you actually can rub the bait up and down all sides of a stump with the heavy sinker until a fish takes the minnow.

Summer crappie will cooperate any time of the day or night. They don't seem to go on limited feeding sprees for only short periods, rather they are willing to take a minnow any time one comes close. This is a tremendous advantage to the fisherman, and it means they are "ready when you are". Like the father and son on vacation, you can fish during "dead" times of the day when the rest of the family wants to sleep or rest, leaving the more pleasant hours for family adventures ashore.

Crappie are sensitive to light as well as water temperatures. If your lake happens to be relatively shallow, even out on the main channel, it's a good idea to search for structure which provides them with shelter or "shade" underwater. This can be as simple as fishing structure on the opposite side from the location of the sun. And don't forget, crappie will be holding on both sides of the channel, so you may be able to catch them on the least-bright slope better than whichever side is in direct sunlight at a given hour. In the middle of the day when the sun is overhead, fish deeper.

When you discover a particularly good hotspot in

open water, take time to line up some natural landmarks on shore so you can return to the location another day. *Write the information down* on a piece of paper so you don't forget. Fishing open water is totally different from what most fishermen are used to doing, and trying to reposition the boat in the same spot another day is far tougher than you may realize until you try it.

A slight rise in the water level usually sparks fishing, and can be a tip-off on where the fish are holding. Generally, a rise in water level causes the fish to come up in depth a bit. A fall in water level usually makes them go slightly deeper down the slope. A cloudy day will cause the fish to come up in depth also, even in August.

One important thing to remember about caring for your catch in hot weather is to *keep the fish away from water.* Mother Nature has provided fish with some type built-in mechanism which prevents water from soaking through their scales and into their bodies. Once you catch the fish and it dies, those little "body pumps" stop working and the fish will absorb water into its flesh. The result is soggy filets. It's a good idea to place your crappie into an ice chest immediately after catching them to keep them fresh in hot weather. And you should take pains to prevent allowing the fish to contact water in the ice chest, too. Put the ice on the bottom and position a couple of heavy cloth towels on top of the ice. Toss the fish on top of the towels and drain the melted ice water frequently. This insures infinitely better-tasting, more firm tablefare later.

This summer, while your fishing pals are spending

their weekends working around the house or watching TV, get out on the lake and enjoy the easiest and most predictable crappie fishing of the year. Just head for the old river channel in your favorite lake or reservoir, and pitch out some buoys along the slope to mark the route as you work it with a tightline rig. The action is so predictable, you can almost invite the neighbors for a fish fry before you head for the lake!

Catching crappie in August can be summed up by my pal Doug's remark after I showed him what it was all about that first time. He told me, "I was wrong, Buck. You're not crazy; it's all those people who sit at home all summer thinking they can't catch crappie in hot weather. *They* are the ones who are crazy!"

Stripers

Sonar expertise plays a huge part in striper fishing success. This species roams the lake almost constantly, and documented studies have shown certain fish sporting little radio transmitters traveled over 20 miles up or down a lake in only a matter of days! On the other hand, I have found stripers on or near the same structure for many days in succession. It may have been a seasonal change in their travel plans, or maybe the structure was so appealing that a new school moved in every time an old one left. I can't say which.

Stripers are very structure-oriented just like other game fish, even though they often cruise the big, open-water areas in a lake. Here the fish probably are

Jack Ray displays what good sonar technique is all about.

following the old river channel, despite the fact it may be 50 or 100 feet below.

Stripers also have a habit of intimidating schools of shad, literally "herding" them into a cove or pocket somewhere, then chopping them up viciously on a feeding spree. At these times, structure may not enter the picture in relation to what is *beneath* the fish, but water depth and the ability to confine their prey becomes important. When stripers chase baitfish into a shallow part of the lake to feed, you can see the surface action from quite a distance. And when you find yourself in the middle of a feeding school like that, it sounds as if someone is throwing concrete blocks into the water. The first time you experience this, you may fear for the safety of small children in the boat.

You can tie on almost any old lure you like and feed it to the fish, as long as the action stays frantic. Topwater enthusiasts go absolutely bananas over this sort of thing.

Finding a ravenous school of stripers reducing the shad population in shallow water is indeed fun. But it happens only rarely to the fisherman who has to work for a living. The great majority of your fish probably will be taken from April to September by using live bait techniques. You find the school with your sonar, position the boat over them with the trolling motor, and fish straight down. In warm weather the fish may be cruising at about 15-to-20-feet below the surface. In hot weather they often go much deeper. I have caught them at depths of 50 feet.

Where legal, live bream are very popular for spring

and summer striper fishing bait. Shiners and goldfish work well, too. And below many dams, you can employ a long-handle net to scoop shad for bait, as they often swim in huge schools along the bank when the utility people are generating power. If a striper is even slightly hungry, he will smack a shad presented to his nose. Bream are probably the next best choice for bait.

The trick is to use your depthfinder in locating the stripers, then place your bait at exactly the depth where they are, keeping it there with the help of a lead sinker a foot or two above the hook. If the fish signals from the school are showing up at 20 feet on your unit, you want that bait to be exactly 20 feet under the transducer. Many live-bait striper fisherman wrap colored thread around their fishing rods a measured 12 inches from the face of their reel. Using the 12-inch mark on the rod, they strip out line with their hand, counting the feet until the desired depth for the bait has been reached. It works beautifully.

If you have a good depthfinder, and if there is very little wind or current to pull your line to the side, you can *watch* your bait go down through the cone of the transducer. You don't have to count out the distance for accuracy; just let the bait fall in the water as you watch it on the depthfinder. When it reaches the fish, you can see it has arrived and engage the reel. Obviously, if you do not drop your bait down through the path of the transducer cone, you can't watch it fall.

Live bait fishing becomes something of a chore if the fish are not hungry. You can stay on top of them half the day and never get a strike. Fortunately, those

Live bait fishing for stripers can pay big dividends if you use your depthfinder to locate them and fish the correct depth.

situations are somewhat rare. Even if the school is not taking offers, there usually are a few mean and aggressive characters down there who will whack your bait just for the pure hell of killing it.

Live bait fishing also offers you your best shot at taking stripers on ultra-light tackle. The idea may sound a bit incredulous in light of how these fish behave when hooked, but if your depthfinder shows no trees or other brush below when stripers are found, you might pull it off. I must confess that catching stripers on ultra-light tackle is a passion of mine. Few things match the thrill and challenge.

If you really want to test your skills with rod and reel, spool up some light line on a small outfit and take a crack at getting a striper in the boat with it. You must be sure there are no underwater structures nearby that can cause problems for the light line. Examine the bottom carefully with your depthfinder, increasing the sensitivity a bit. Placing a sharp hook into a striper's mouth seems to give him an almost uncontrollable urge to tie monofilament knots around branches.

Vertical jigging for stripers can produce excellent tablefare, also. Almost any of the rectangular metal jigs or lead spoons will work quite well, providing they have sufficient weight to be worked effectively. A chunk of pork rind sometimes gives the lure more appeal. Other lures, like lead-heads with plastic tails, will produce, also. In fact, I caught a World Record striper vertical jigging with a lure like that.

My fishing pal Jack Ray and I were fishing in Norris Lake during October. We found a few stripers holding

*Weighing over 45 pounds, this striper would make
any angler proud.*

quite deep, and began trying to entice them with a five-inch Sassy Shad. The lure is heavy, has a soft, flexible tail, and is well-suited to the effort. The action was not very spectacular until we decided to leave.

The fish Jack had spotted on his sonar were right near the bottom in 52-foot water. After only limited success at this particular location, Jack was ready to move and suggested we reel up our lines. I took a couple of cranks on my reel and the line stopped coming up. It began going out.

Norris Lake is clear and deep. An old lake in the TVA chain, its trees and stump rows have long since gone the way of the dinosaurs, leaving the lake bottom clean and snag-free. Jack is also an ultralight fan when it comes to stripers, and we were taking advantage of the lake conditions. I believe Jack was using either four or six-pound line. I was using eight-pound stuff on a spanking new rod and reel fresh from the box.

When the fish took my departing jig, I set the hook and the fun began. More accurately, the waiting began. It's hard to get a striper's full attention when you can't exert a great deal of pressure because of light line. Granted, eight-pound line is barely considered to be in the ultra-light family, but this was a case where my initial concern was finding out the prowess of my new equipment. I saw no reason to break off fish with the lighter line while learning how far I could push the stress factor on the new gear.

Anyhow, after the fish had taken us on a tour of the lower end of the lake, he tired of the game and began to fight. Jack and I both knew from the way he acted that

*Author holds up his World Record Striper taken on eight-pound
line in Norris Lake, Tennessee.*

this was a good fish. He was heavy, and he stayed well down in the water. After much sweat in the October crispness, I got the striper to the surface, where he rolled like a walrus in a feather bed.

We eased the boat over to the fish carefully as I kept the rod high and the line tight. (One does not drag a big fish across the water to one's boat when one is using light line, unless one wishes to hear one's line say "ping".) The fish was boated, and his length exceeded the width of Jack's big bass boat. He lay there with his nose jammed against the rod compartment on one side of the boat and his tail curled up the gunwale on the other. Nice fish.

The fish weighed 34 pounds, 1 ounce after Jack insisted I remove my thumb from the scales. It was a World Record for freshwater stripers on eight-pound line.

Topwater fishing for stripers generates enough excitement to last a lifetime. It also calls for nerves of steel and good fishing techniques. Unfortunately, it's addictive, and once you have experienced the thrill, you'll keep going back for more again and again. Take for example, the trip I made with two clients on a large reservoir last year in late spring:

In the pre-dawn mist, we could hear stripers exploding the surface nearly 300 yards away. It sounded much like someone had climbed a tall tree on the bank and was throwing building blocks into the water. A large group of stripers had herded a thick school of shad into a

Big stripers at daybreak strip line, fight hard.

cove in six-foot water, and was going about their routine
business of chopping them up into bite-size chunks.
The surface was filled with activity; we could make out
big splashes sending water skyward for two feet or more
as I eased the boat into position on the edge of the
melee.

Before stopping the boat to begin casting oversized
surface lures at the fish, I again explained the procedure
to my pair of fishermen. We rechecked the knots in their
line, made sure there were no nicks or abrasions in the
mono, and tested the drag on each reel. I knew it would
do little good, but I cautioned them again not to attempt
to set the hook until they actually *felt* the fish hit the
lure. Then I turned the boat sideways to the feeding
school and told them to have at it.

On his first cast, one of the chaps had a hit almost
immediately after the lure hit the water. His reel began
whizzing loudly as line peeled off the spool. The guy
almost fell out of the boat trying to regain his balance
after being forcefully pulled forward by the strike!

While the one man fought his fish, the other made
another cast or two out to the left and away from the
hooked fish. He was excited, reeling the big stickbait
too fast, and I suggested he slow it down to make only a
small "V" wake on the surface. He did that, and before
he turned the crank another four or five times, a huge
striper made a violent pass, erupting in a shower of
water right behind the guy's lure. Even though the fish
had hit at least a foot behind the lure, the man heaved
back on his rod with all his strength, sending the treble-
hook-armed lure sailing through the air right at the boat.

Ducking treble hooks is one of the less pleasant things a striper guide must learn to do when topwater fishing with inexperienced clients.

Big lures, big fish and big thrills; that's what topwater striper fishing is all about. There are some things you should know about how to find schools of feeding stripers, and a few more things about how to boost your chances of getting one into the boat. Probably the main reason for failing to find these heavy-duty brawlers comes from not spending enough time on the lake looking for them. Stripers typically feed very actively early and late in the day when they find shad in schools over relatively shallow water. Too many fishermen merely go out on the lake and cruise around looking for action on the surface. If they don't happen to be motoring by an area when the fish surface, they don't know what to do, and return home unsuccessful.

Stripers are very structure-oriented. They hang out in the deeper waters of large lakes and reservoirs, but do so in direct relation to structure well below them. Often you'll find them along the old river channel out in the middle of the lake, even though the water is perhaps 100 feet deep, and the fish are suspended at 15 or 20 feet right above the shoulder of the channel. In the warmer months, stripers normally feed in more shallow areas at least part of the day. The hotter the weather, the shorter the surface/shallow-water feeding duration, and the earlier and later in the day it occurs.

If you can't find a fishing buddy who will tell you the truth about where the fish are hitting topwater, or a dock operator on the lake who knows the straight poop, you can fall back on your depthfinder and the knowledge of how stripers relate to structure. A good topo map of the lake will save you a great deal of time in narrowing down the possibilities of where the action is most likely to occur. Look for shallow flats of 12 feet or less which are located adjacent to deep drop-offs where the old river channel is found maybe 50 feet or more below. These are good spots for the fish to move up shallow for a short feeding spree, then move back down in depth during the hot portion of the day.

Run the boat to a potential area such as that, then use the depthfinder to search for large fish on the edge of the drop-off(s). If stripers are present, and ready to feed on the surface, you should see a few swirls on the water as you approach. If the action is already underway, of course, you'll find explosive action like I described in the beginning story about my two clients on their first trip.

If the fish can be spotted on sonar, but don't appear to be ready to feed on the surface, don't worry. I've seen stripers come rocketing up from 12 or 14 feet below to smack a big topwater plug pulled slowly overhead! Sometimes the fish are ready to feed, but the shad aren't around in number, so most of the activity occurs beneath the surface where you don't see it happening. Under those circumstances, stripers will blast a topwater plug with equal enthusiasm as when feeding in a visible frenzy.

It's best not to run the big engine on your boat directly over the fish in water less than 35 feet deep. The trick is to motor out to a potential holding area near the

*Use your LCD to find underwater ridges and humps
others miss.*

deep drop-offs, then use the trolling motor to search for them with your depthfinder. Stripers are a bit boat-shy after the season gets going, and sometimes spook rather easily when a prop-exhaust motor churns water over their heads. Once you have determined stripers are present in the flats, back the boat away to the maximum distance you can cast a large topwater lure without having to strain your tackle.

Cast into the area you want to work (either amid a feeding school chopping up shad on the surface, or a holding area where nothing can be seen on top other than an occasional swirl or two), and retrieve the bait *slowly* across the surface. You don't want to put any excess action into the lure. It's supposed to look like an injured shad, an easy meal for the striper. Six or seven-inch shallow-running lures are best, and you should put an "O-ring" into the lure eye, creating a slightly larger wobble on the slow retrieve. The lure is retrieved just fast enough to make a "V" wake on top of the water. It should not be reeled in fast enough to sink below the surface. The action of the slow wobble on the surface drives stripers wild! Don't try to add action with jerks, darts and dives created by pumping the rod tip. Slow, deliberate retrieves are far more productive on top 90 percent of the time.

My choice of line is around the 16-pound mark with tough, flexible mono like TriLene Blue. I normally rig up tackle for my clients using 20 or 25-pound mono, as I feel it increases their chances of landing the big fish once hooked, even though it may limit their casting distance somewhat. Some of the boat-for-hire cowboys

Understanding sonar readout is the key to better fishing today.
It takes practice.

who guide on my local waters for stripers use 35 or
40-pound line for their customers, but I personally
believe that's a bit much for casting with any degree of
distance, and you'll spook the school if you get overly
close to the action.

Hooks on the jumbo lures *must* be sharpened on a
stone prior to going out on the water. Even spanking
new lures right out of the box need a few touches with a
stone to put a razor edge on the points of the treble
hooks, and it makes a material difference in success
over the long run. Dull hooks lose fish. Sharp ones
make it possible to show off your catch afterwards!

A reel with easily adjustable drag is best for
topwater use. Set the drag loosely initially, as a striper
smashes the lure with violent malice and strength. You
can use your thumb on a bait-casting reel to stop the
surge momentarily and set the hook firmly, or use your
finger to do the same on a heavy-duty spinning outfit.
Once the fish is securely hooked and raising h. . . on the
line, you merely tighten the drag slightly and begin the
chore of wearing him down using both reel drag and rod
action. There's no point in "pumping" a freshly-hooked
striper. Just hold on and let him run against the drag
and the bend in your rod. Don't make the mistake of
cranking down the drag system too tightly, as this will
only result in the fish breaking your line.

Those who have caught stripers before by using live
bait or vertical jigging techniques when the fish were
20 feet or more beneath the boat will have a genuine
surprise in store when topwater fishing for them. A big
striper hooked on topwater will actually *jump* like a

bass when you stick him. I've had stripers in the 30-pound class come shooting out of the water three or four feet high after feeling the steel hook in their jaw! And they did it *three or four times* before taking on the more typical antics of power-diving and surging against the reel heading for deeper waters. Talk about excitement! When the fish comes up, "bow" the rod to him, allowing the slack to cushion the sudden increase of pressure on the line when he lands and runs again.

Perhaps the one key to successful topwater striper fishing once you find them, is *patience*. It often takes several casts over a school to generate a strike, and often those strikes are short, missing the lure by a foot or more. I have no idea why stripers frequently miss the bait by such margins, but it might be in an effort to determine if the lure is actually a live shad or not. Regardless of the reason the fish do this, it's up to the fisherman not to snatch the lure back to the boat when a striper hits short, thus removing the lure from his reach. This is where the "nerves of steel" come into play. If you *feel* the fish hit the bait, you can set the hook. If there is a huge splash near your lure, but you don't actually feel the jolt on your line, you should instantly stop the retrieve and let the lure sit still in the water for a couple of seconds. When you begin the retrieve again, it's very likely the fish will hit it a second time, nailing the lure with full force. Training yourself to do this is much harder to do than read about it! It *is* necessary for success, however.

If you're lucky enough to find big stripers churning the surface as they feed on shad, you'll have little or no

*Topwater striper action is an experience you'll never forget.
Even when they aren't spotted on the surface, you can find
likely places for heavy-duty brawls by using your LCD to locate
flats near river channel drop-offs.*

trouble catching them by pulling a large lure slowly through the turmoil. If you don't find surface action you can see, you can catch them handily by using a depth-finder and topo map to search the potential areas on your favorite lake. Either way, topwater striper fishing will be the most exciting flavor of fishing excitement you have ever encountered, and that's a sure and certain fact.

Be sure you have good line without nicks in it, a good drag system on your reel, and the patience to let the fish take the lure physically before you set the hook. Let the fish run against the reel until he slows, then tighten the drag *slightly* to put more pressure on him. A fresh, or "green" striper in the 25-pound class will strip out 75 yards of line in less time than it will take you to ask your spouse to get the Ben-Gay to rub on your aching muscles that night. Retrieve the lure slowly over the school, no matter how intense the excitement of seeing the surface erupting in explosions of spray when the fish are feeding. And be prepared to come into work late every day during the peak season for topwater striper fishing, as it will get into your blood and you'll find the need to be on the water at daybreak much more appealing than going into the office for some silly meeting with the boss. Of course, if you're one of the few, fortunate souls who has a boss you like, you could introduce *him* (or her) to topwater striper fishing one morning, and you'll not have to worry again about being late for work!

6
Concluding Thoughts On Liquid Crystal Units

Development of the LCD may well go in the books as one of the most important advances in the sonar industry ever to come off the planning boards. You can be certain there are many more new and unique developments on the way, all designed to provide more information for fishermen and boaters. Yet the greatest advantage one has when operating LCD machines is the pure simplicity of the readout. As dozens of additional bells and whistles are sure to be added to existing units in the future, one must stop and wonder where it is all going.

When the original flasher units came onto the market, they were hailed as the "ultimate fish finder," and anglers used them happily to find large structure below, taking note they also were able to know the exact depth of that structure, too. Circuitry was improved, and it became easier to spot fish signals showing up on the dial. Multiple depth scales were added, improved transducers with a variety of cone angles were marketed. Then along came paper graphs, again hailed as the "ultimate". The growth and improvements in paper graphs was much faster. By the time a chap learned how to use his machine, there were four more models out on the market, all of which provided better detail, had maybe a half-dozen new features, and cost twice as much. The final generation of paper graphs are so sophisticated they generate a staggering amount of information, and it takes years to fully master their full potential for the average user. It's worth noting one of the prime reasons for the overnight popularity of LCD units was due to their ease of interpretation, and their more moderate price tags.

With each model year since LCD was first marketed, the units have sported more sophistication, more pixels, more features, and higher costs on the dealer shelf. It will be interesting to watch the race between manufacturers in this new arena. There is little doubt LCD units will be improved time and again until they reach the maximum balance mark between performance and reasonable cost. And even as you read this, there are highly-skilled engineers working on totally new and different concepts which will become the *next* "ultimate" in depthfinders!

Regarding LCD units, their advancement in performance has indeed been rapid, and may be approach-

All species of fish, from bream to lake trout, lend themselves to sonar use for improved success.

ing that "balance" between cost and effectiveness. There presently are units featuring over 2,000 pixels per square inch on the screen, and that seems about the maximum possible coverage before the cost to manufacture becomes exorbitant. Any LCD screen with 1,800 pixels or more per square inch has full ability to draw out nice curves for you. There are units which are combined with Loran C operation, and even have a memory to record your "honey holes" for later use in returning to the spot. Problems with the rainbow effect on some screens when you wear polarized sunglasses are being resolved, and have been greatly reduced. You can even buy LCD units which make the fish signals flash or turn a different color, if you like that sort of thing.

At some point, it is logical you will wave the towel and say "enough". There will be one depthfinder which has performed well for you, one that you have mastered and that serves you well under the conditions you most-often encounter when fishing. That's the unit you will stay with, foregoing the trade shows every spring where all the newest electronic goodies are brightly displayed, and ignoring the wonderfully packaged units backed with $350,000 advertising campaigns. It will be like finding the shotgun with a perfect fit for your stance and dropping doubles on every covey rise. You will stop looking for a better weapon and begin enjoying the one you have more fully.

There is only one effective way to reach the point of satisfaction with depthfinder units, regardless of the type, style or price. You must devote sufficient hours

Healthy largemouth taken from deep stumprow near bridge.

on the water using the unit to prove or disprove the unit's ability to meet your personal needs for fishing information. There are no shortcuts to learning about everything your unit is capable of doing for you. Unfortunately, a great many anglers never work hard enough with their depthfinders to learn everything it will do for them.

I surely cannot tell you what an "adequate" amount of time would be for you to spend working with your depthfinder in an attempt to master its full potential. The material offered in this book is sufficient for you to use in the process, and should cut the time requirement substantially. Yet it may still take a year or more before you can say with authority that your machine fits the bill in every respect. It took me *five* years of hard research before I was able to write my first book on using depthfinders, and I already knew how to type before starting!

It cannot be overemphasized: you must take the time to spend on the water with your depthfinder which is necessary for you to become skilled in its use. The LCD machines go a very long way in making interpretation of signals rather easy to do, and they are a blessing for most anglers as a result. Your liquid crystal display depthfinder might just be the machine you decide to keep forever and begin enjoying. But discovering this fact becomes a matter of how much time you are willing to give it during the learning process.

Good luck!

Credits

Wayne Curtis
design and layout

Buck Taylor
cover art

Bailey Typography, Inc.
Nashville, Tennessee
typesetting

Lithographics, Inc.
Nashville, Tennessee
printing

Additional copies of this book are available from:

OUTDOOR SKILLS BOOKSHELF
P.O. Box 13
Louisville, AL 36048

Other books by the author:

THE COMPLETE GUIDE TO USING DEPTHFINDERS,
Revised Ed. 258 pages fully illustrated, $9.95. Explains
in great detail exactly how to use your depthfinder to its
maximum potential for fishing, covering the subject
from "A to Z" in straight-talking, information-packed
terms. Considered the standard reference source on
depthfinder usage today, this book is in its tenth printing
due to demand. Basic and advanced principles of
correct way to get maximum results with flashers,
graphs and LCDs, plus many illustrations using actual
graph paper readings. Highly endorsed by pros and
manufacturers. "Must reading" for all depthfinder
owners. Easy to understand and fun to read.

Buck Taylor's PRACTICAL GUIDE TO CATCHING
MORE CRAPPIE. 228 pages fully illustrated, $9.95.
Gives far more information than any other similar book
on the market, providing details that take crappie in
every month of the year. Tactics, tackle, use of
depthfinders, even cleaning and cooking are covered in
informative, valuable chapters designed to make you a
more successful crappie fisherman. Explains how
crappie migrate in large lakes, and how to find and catch
them every day of the year.

Order from:
OUTDOOR SKILLS BOOKSHELF
Post Office Box 13
Louisville, AL 36048

osb